For the Sea Life Sanctuary rescue team.
You are heroes. – SD

For Lucie – AT

SAVING SHARK PUP

The incredible true story

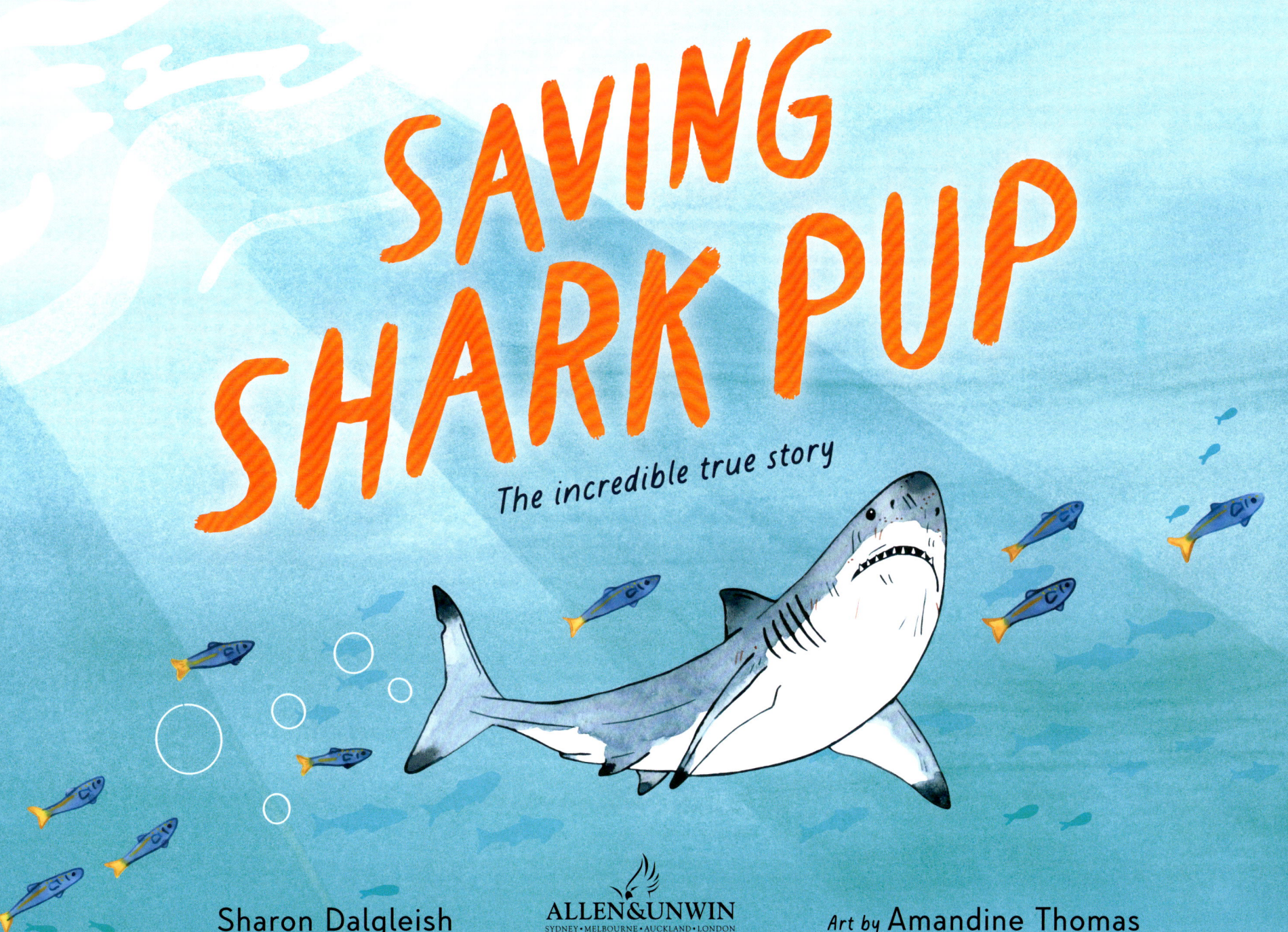

Sharon Dalgleish

ALLEN&UNWIN
SYDNEY · MELBOURNE · AUCKLAND · LONDON

Art by Amandine Thomas

Far from the sandy shore,
a great white shark is born.

He swims away from his mother.

Great white shark mothers leave their babies as soon as they are born. The pups must immediately fend for themselves.

The ocean provides
everything shark pup needs.

Silently, he cruises the currents of his wild, deep world.

Newborn pups are about 1.5 metres long – as long as a bathtub.
An adult great white shark can measure up to 6 metres.

Alone, he explores and grows until one day something grabs him…

SURF!

The sounds and smells of shark pup's world turn upside down.

Waves fling him against rocks.

Then snatch and tumble and spit him...

When a shark is upside down, it can go into a trance-like state, where its muscles relax and it becomes disoriented.

onto the sand.

People come closer, concerned.

Slowly, they drag shark pup out past the breaking surf.

It is not far enough.
The waves tumble again
and wash him back to shore.

Lifeguards arrive. But they rescue people, not sharks.

Great white sharks can swim up to 55 kilometres per hour and dive 1200 metres deep. They don't usually get caught in the surf.

At last, divers rush in with a net and chain-mail gloves.

Everyone works together to drag shark pup to deeper water.

Shark scales feel like sandpaper. Chain-mail gloves protect the divers' hands.

Shark pup tries to swim. It's the wrong direction! He smashes against rocks.

His snout and body scratch and scrape.

The divers don't give up. This time, they use the net to lift shark pup up, away from the ocean and everything he knows.

They need somewhere safe to put shark pup, while they make a plan to return him home.

They carry him along the beach, running, stumbling,

The divers used a scissor net to transport shark pup. When he swam towards the net, the divers closed the poles so that the net surrounded him.

towards an ocean pool packed with people.

Children clamber out so shark pup can take their place.

The net lowers. His gills move. He breathes in the water.

But his senses are scrambled.
This is not his wild, deep world.

He doesn't know which way to swim.

Sharks have electroreceptors that detect electrical and magnetic signals. The metal in the swimming pool distorted these signals and made shark pup lose his sense of direction.

Chain-mail gloves gently turn shark pup from hard edges, tight corners and shallow spaces.

A crowd grows. Cameras click. Everyone wants to get close to a great white shark.

Shark pup's fin droops.

Sharks have been around since the time of dinosaurs, but most people will never encounter a great white shark.

People offer snacks and drinks to the cold, tired divers.
'We need sunglasses,' the divers call back, as late
afternoon sunshine glares across the water.

Under rippling shadows, it is harder to see shark pup.
It is harder to help him. He slams into concrete walls.

Great white sharks cannot survive in captivity. Even in the ocean, they do not stay in the same area for long.

Gloved hands hold firm to calm him as the tub is loaded onto a ute.

There is only the swoosh, bump of the tub.

Shark pup's fin droops lower.

A team of divers from Sea Life Sanctuary cared for shark pup. Their knowledge was the key to shark pup's rescue.

Suddenly, more water. Deep water.
It is only an ocean water storage tank,
but shark pup can rest here for tonight.

Divers are with him. No rest for them.
They stay all night in the water.

They watch shark pup swim.
They watch his gills move,
make sure he is still breathing.

The tank at Sea Life Sanctuary was circular, larger and much deeper than the pool.

Morning arrives, bringing more gloves that poke and prod.

Shark pup received injections of antibiotics to fight infections and vitamins to reduce stress.

Then, the net lifts.

It hauls shark pup up, past clanging metal…

and quickly outside to a waiting boat.

Shark pup is trapped again in that tub so tight.

The world turns to wind and
speed and the smell of diesel.
A diver bends into the tub, working
to keep water and gills moving.

The oxygen levels in the tub were higher than normal to keep shark pup calm.

Though shark pup cannot see the ocean, he can smell it. Shark pup is calm. It is time.

SWIM, SHARK PUP, SWIM!

The ocean seems to sigh.

Two divers are with him still. Watching. Willing him. *Swim, shark pup, swim.*

AUTHOR'S NOTE

This book is a true story about a great white shark pup that washed up on Manly Beach, Sydney, in September 2017. As the local community rushed to witness the rescue, a young boy in the crowd named the pup Fluffy. The shark pup was 1.8 metres long and the rescuers thought he might have been three to five years old. They decided not to tag the shark pup with a tracking device before they released him. They did not want to cause him any more distress. We will never know for sure if he survived. But we will always have hope. For Fluffy and for all the ocean's sharks.

First published by Allen & Unwin in 2026

Copyright © Text, Sharon Dalgleish 2026
Copyright © Illustrations, Amandine Thomas 2026

All rights reserved. No part of this book may be reproduced or transmitted in any form or by any means, electronic or mechanical, including photocopying, recording or by any information storage and retrieval system, without prior permission in writing from the publisher. The Australian Copyright Act 1968 (the Act) allows a maximum of one chapter or ten per cent of this book, whichever is the greater, to be photocopied by any educational institution for its educational purposes provided that the educational institution (or body that administers it) has given a remuneration notice to the Copyright Agency (Australia) under the Act.

Allen & Unwin
Cammeraygal Country
83 Alexander Street
Crows Nest NSW 2065
Australia
Phone: (61 2) 8425 0100
Email: info@allenandunwin.com
Web: www.allenandunwin.com

Allen & Unwin acknowledges the Traditional Owners of the Country on which we live and work. We pay our respects to all Aboriginal and Torres Strait Islander Elders, past and present.

EU Authorised Representative: Easy Access System Europe,
Mustamäe tee 50, 10621 Tallinn, Estonia,
gpsr.requests@easproject.com

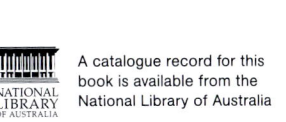 A catalogue record for this book is available from the National Library of Australia

ISBN 978 1 76118 201 3

For teaching resources, explore allenandunwin.com/learn

Thank you to aquarist Hope Nugent for spending over twenty-four hours in the water with shark pup, for answering all my questions, and for reviewing and checking the manuscript. – Sharon

Illustrations created with watercolour using a brush and dip-pen on Bristol and tracing paper, and assembled digitally.

Cover and text design by Kristy Lund-White
Set in 19 pt Pani Sans Medium by Kristy Lund-White

This book was printed in October 2025 in China by C&C Offset Printing Co. Ltd.

10 9 8 7 6 5 4 3 2 1

www.sharondalgleishbooks.com
www.amandine-thomas.com

MIX
Paper | Supporting responsible forestry
FSC® C008047